science process

D1798859

Be scientific

Contents

Theme 1

Symbols you will find:

▶ These are things you should try to do.

▶ These are extra things to do if you have time.

◆ These are questions to think about when you are planning practical work.

⚠ When you see this symbol you need to take extra care.

This theme contains 15 spreads which can be worked through in any order.

Discussing

When you are learning, it is very important to talk to other people and discuss things. This helps you to get your ideas clear in your head. Scientists often discuss their work with each other, and you need to do this in your work.

You will learn a lot from listening and talking to each other. Talking and listening are an essential part of everything you do in **Science in Process**. You will usually work in groups of three or four people.

Discuss

▶ Get into a group of three or four. Do Cut Out BS1 (part 1). Make sure you try to do all the things in the picture below.

Record

▶ Write down the order you decide on – you will need it later.

Discuss

▶ Discuss each point in this checklist. How good was your group at discussing?

Did everyone get a turn to say what they thought?
Did everyone listen to each other's point of view?
Did everyone have something to do?
Did everyone agree with the decisions the group made?
How did you come to a decision? (Vote, agreement...?)
How could you improve next time?

Discuss

▶ Ask your teacher for Cut Out BS1 (part 2). This has information about how much electricity each appliance uses.

▶ Now discuss in your group the order for the cut strips that you decided on before. Do you want to change it now that you have this information?

▶ Go through the discussing checklist again. Have you got any better at discussing?

Record

▶ Record your new order.
▶ Record any ways you have got better at discussing.

Discuss

▶ If you wanted to reduce your electricity bill, which appliances would you use less often?
▶ Imagine you are moving to a place where you can only get 50 units of electricity a day. If you could take five appliances with you, which ones would you take and why?

Planning

When you are using **Science in Process** you will often be asked to plan, or follow a plan. 'Follow the plan' means you will have instructions to follow. 'Plan' means you will have to decide how to do the activity yourselves. Use the flow charts to learn how to plan your science work.

How to follow a plan

Read all the information given and look at the diagrams. Watch out for any care symbols ⚠

⬇

Discuss what you are trying to find out. What do you already know that will help you?

⬇

Make sure you understand what to do. There may be exact instructions, or there may be practical questions with a ◆ symbol to help you.

⬇

Make sure you read the **Record** before you start. What does it want you to do? What notes will you make to help you?

⬇

Decide what equipment you need.

⬇

Share out the jobs for this activity in your group.

⬇

Now do the activity.

⬇

If you can, try any activities with a ▶ symbol.

Follow the plan

You can use a circuit with a light bulb and battery to test whether materials let electricity through. This is called 'conduction'. If the bulb lights up then the material conducts electricity. You may find Skill Sheet 3 helpful.

Touch the two crocodile clips together to check the circuit. Now put the aluminium foil between the two crocodile clips.

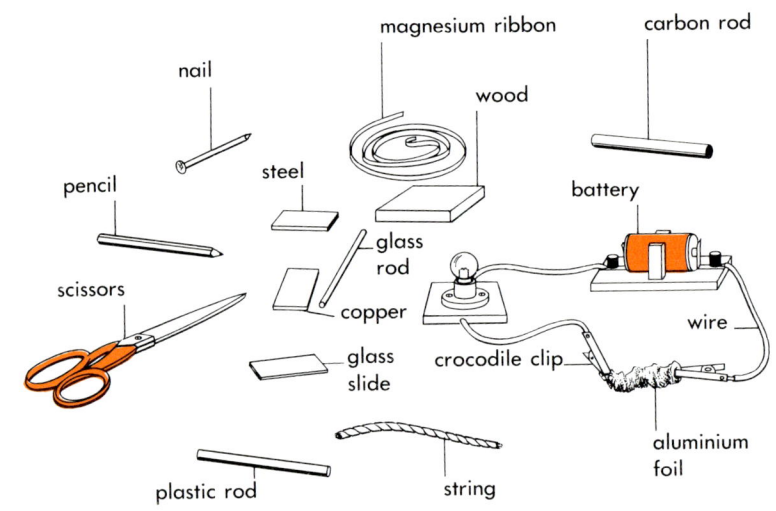

◆ Does the bulb light up?
◆ Does aluminium foil conduct electricity?
◆ What happens to the bulb when you put some of the other materials between the crocodile clips?

▶ Find out which liquids conduct electricity.

Record

▶ Make a list of the materials that conduct electricity.
▶ Make a list of some everyday objects that you think would conduct electricity.

Sometimes you will have to make your own plan and decide how to carry it out. Use this flow chart to help you.

How to make a plan

Discuss what you are trying to find out. What do you already know that will help you?

Decide on a method to use.

Decide what things you can vary or change. Decide which things must stay the same for a test to be fair.

What things are you going to notice or measure?

What senses can you use? Is there any instrument that will help you?

⚠ Is your plan safe? Show it to your teacher.

Decide what you will record.

Now follow your own plan.

If you can, try any activities with a ▶ symbol.

Plan

Some metals fizz when they are put in acids.

Find out which of the metals you have been given fizz the most. This equipment might help you.

◆ What will you record?

Record

▶ Record what your plan was.
▶ Record what you found out.

Recording

You will do a lot of recording in science. You will need to record the things you notice. You may also need to record ideas you have so that you may use them again.

There are a number of ways you can record. The way you choose depends on what you need the recording for.

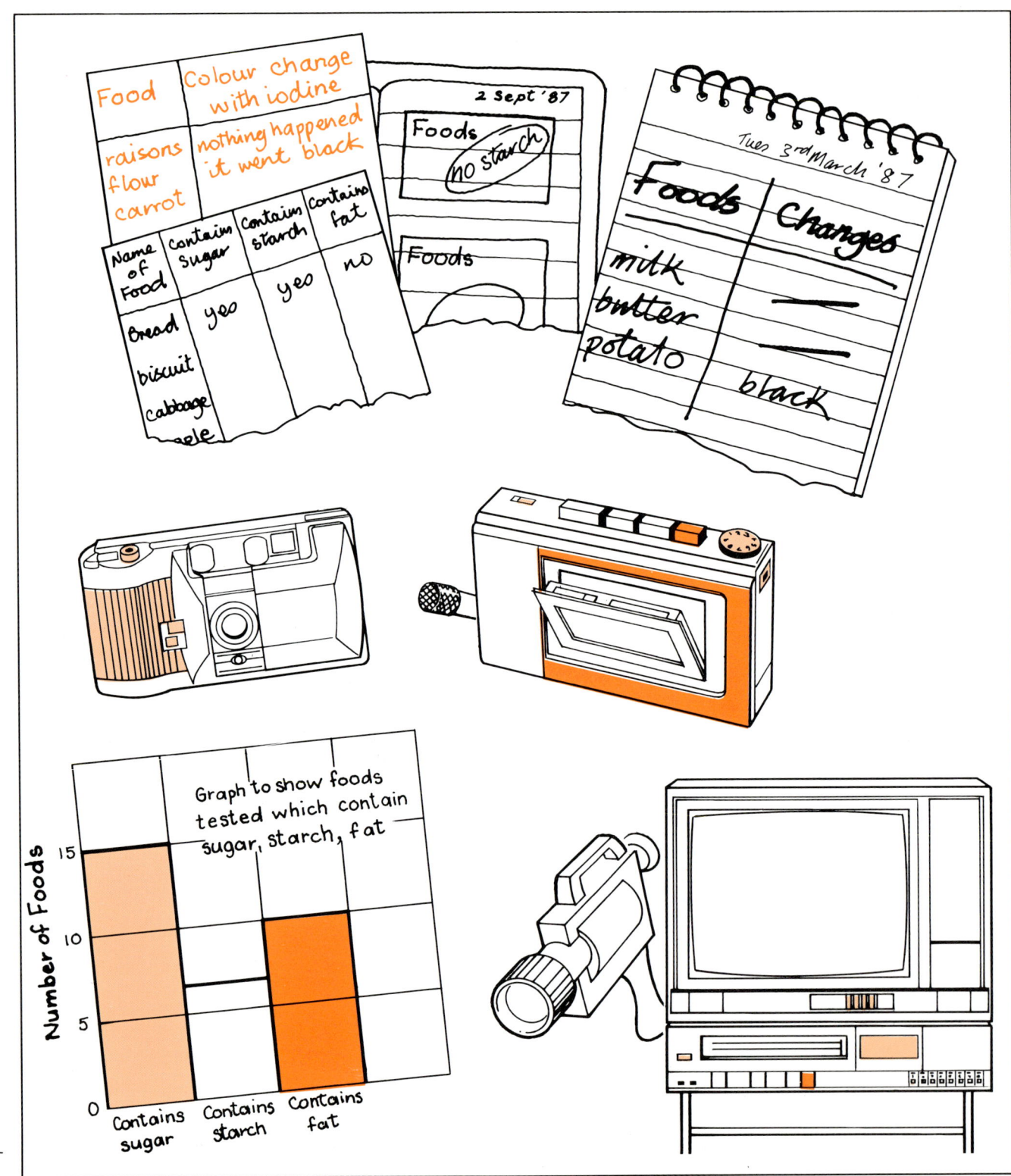

Plan

Your group is going to use the 'iodine test' to find out which foods have starch in them. Starch is a chemical which can give you energy.

Before you start, remember to read the instructions and think about which type of record you might use.

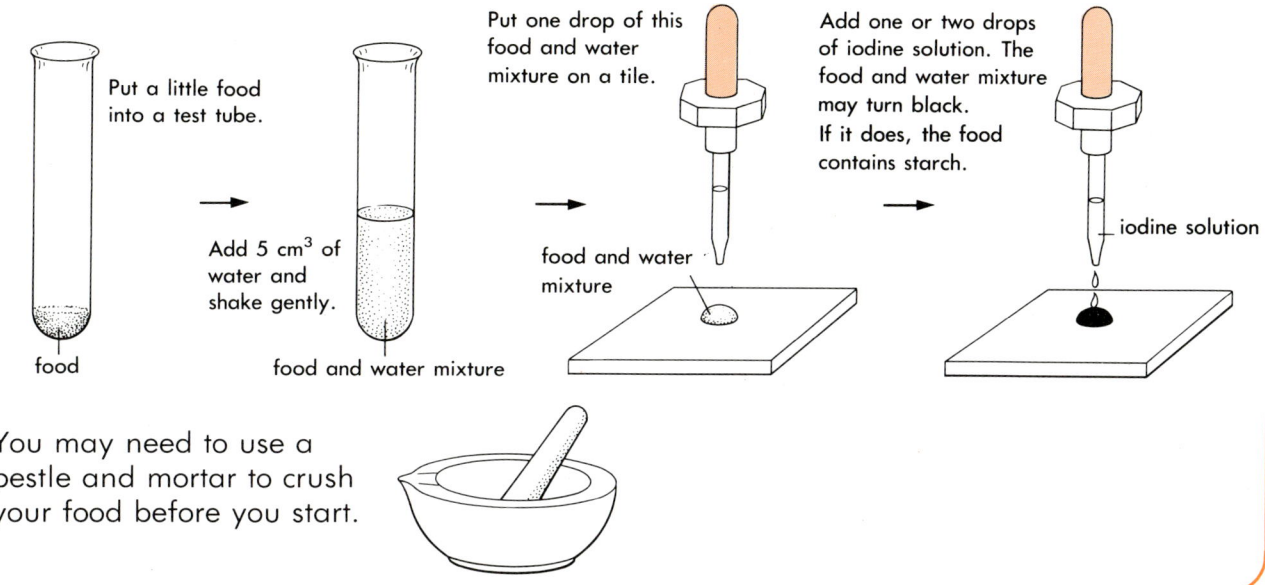

Put a little food into a test tube.

food

Add 5 cm³ of water and shake gently.

food and water mixture

Put one drop of this food and water mixture on a tile.

food and water mixture

Add one or two drops of iodine solution. The food and water mixture may turn black. If it does, the food contains starch.

iodine solution

You may need to use a pestle and mortar to crush your food before you start.

Record

▶ Make a table to show which of the foods you tested had starch in them and which did not.

The recording you have done so far will remind you what happened when you did the iodine test. You may also want to record other ideas or information about your results. To do this you will need to record what you did and what you found out.

Record

What we did
▶ Make a record of what your group did. Use Cut Out BS2 to help you.

What we found out
▶ Look back at the first record you made of your results. Decide what you found out.
▶ Write about 'What we found out'. Use one or both of the ways shown here to help you.
▶ Try other ways of recording.

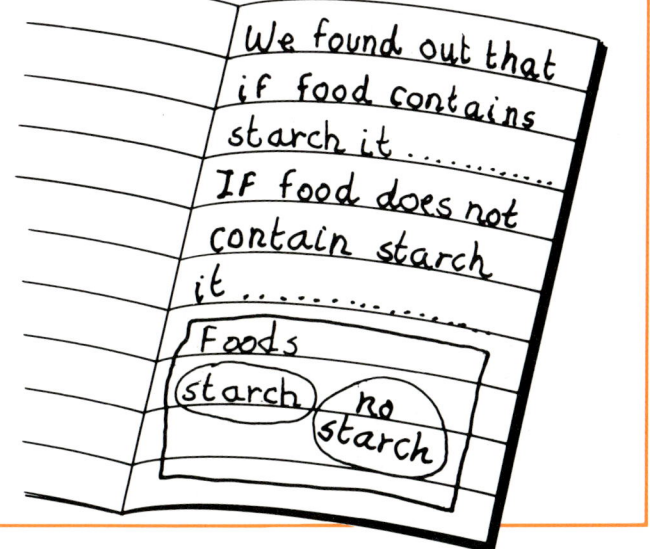

We found out that if food contains starch it ....

If food does not contain starch it ....

Foods
(starch) (no starch)

Presenting

Presenting means showing your ideas and work to other people. You can do this in a variety of ways. For example, you can make posters and charts, design and make models, or write and give a talk. You can write a play or story or poem and perform some of these, or make tapes or songs.

How you present something depends on who your audience is and where you are making your presentation.

Plan

You are going to collect some information about your teeth. You can then present it in different ways.

Use a mirror to look at the teeth in your mouth.

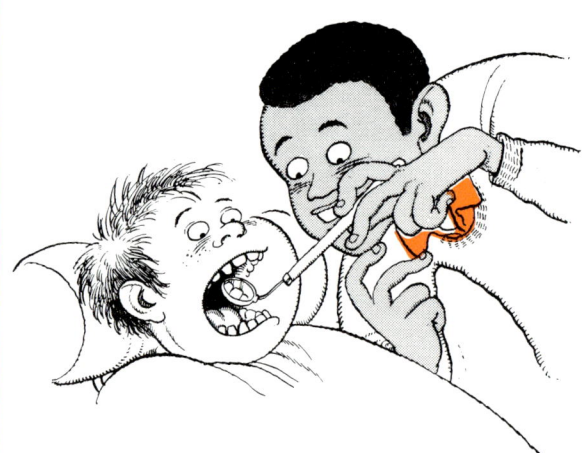

◆ How many teeth have you got altogether?
Look at the types of teeth shown below.
◆ Where in your mouth are your incisors, canines, premolars, and molars?

Imagine you are eating an apple or a piece of bread.

◆ What job do you think each type of tooth does? Some words you can use are: cutting, tearing, grinding, crushing, ripping, biting.

Types of teeth

Record

▶ Make a list of the different jobs each type of tooth does.

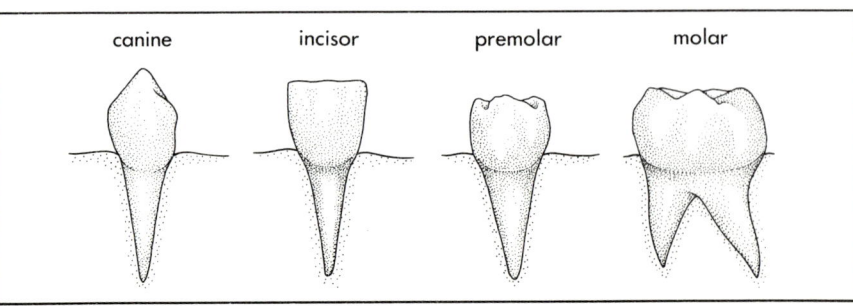

canine   incisor   premolar   molar

Present

▶ Use Cut Out BS3 to make a poster that shows the position of each type of tooth in your mouth. Label each type and colour it.

▶ Choose one or two other ways to present the ideas you have about teeth. There are some ideas shown below.

Before you begin, decide who your audience is and where you are going to present your ideas.

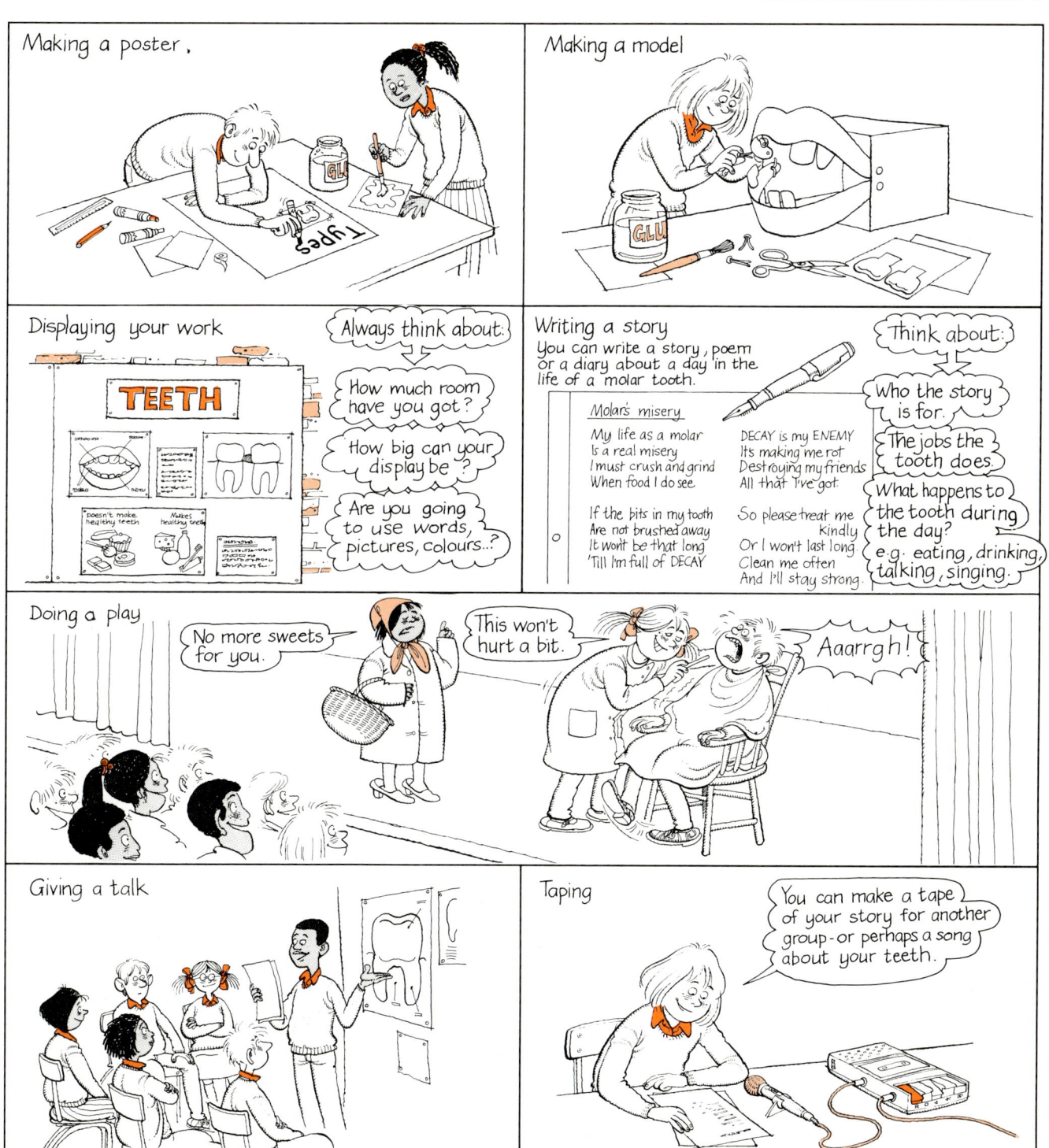

Applying

Applying means using what you know or have found out in a new situation. In this spread you will learn about birds' feet and beaks and then **apply** the information by using it in another situation.

Birds' feet

Read this information. It tells you how birds' feet help them to live in their environment.

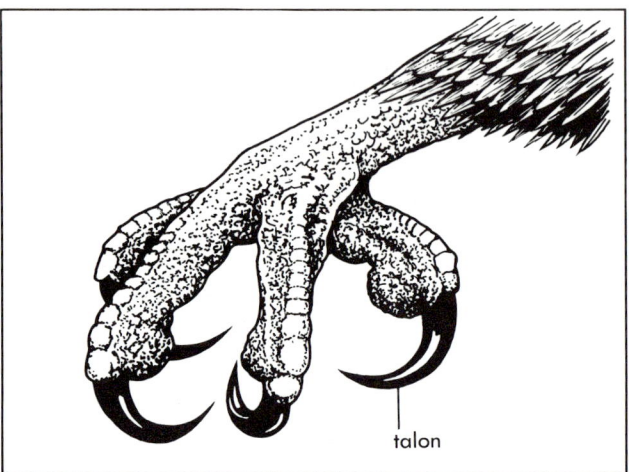

talon

Feet like this belong to a bird of prey. They are used for gripping and killing.

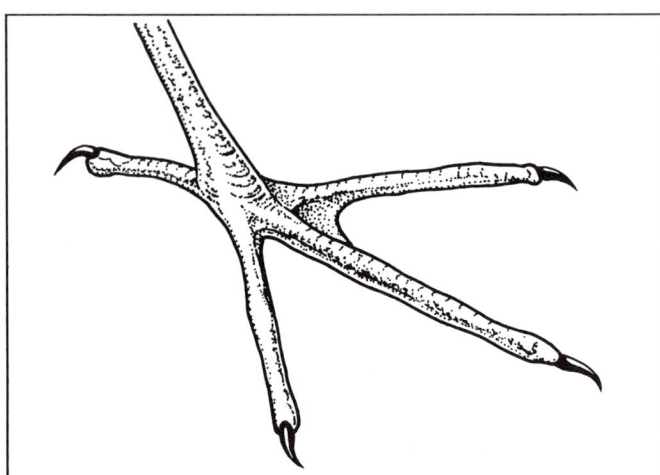

This foot has very long toes with small webs between them. It helps a bird stand on mud.

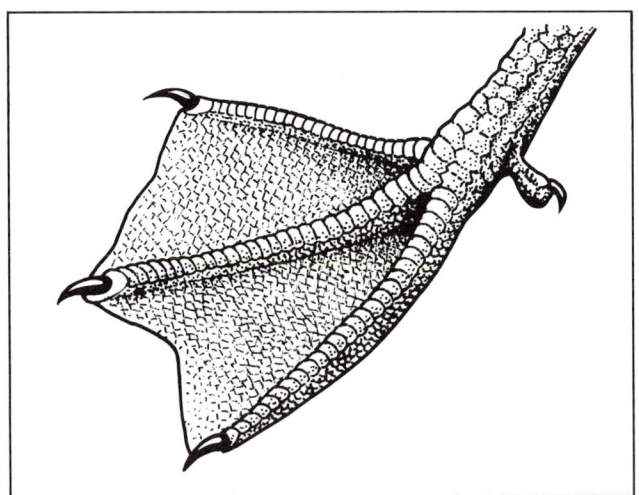

Webbed feet help birds to swim.

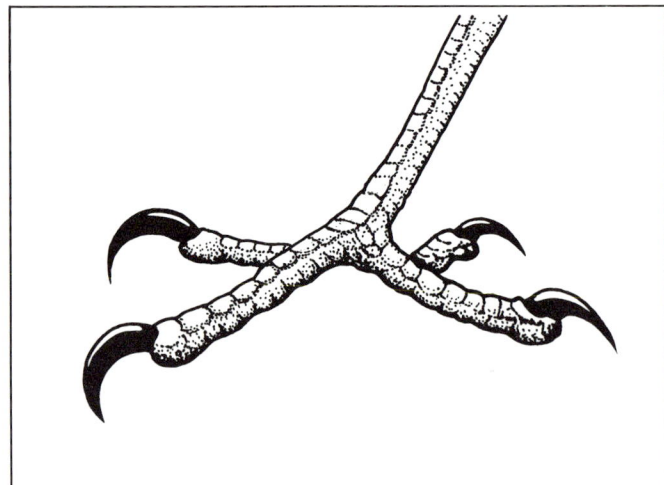

Feet like this one help birds to hold onto trees while they peck their food.

Birds' beaks

Record

▶ Do Cut Out BS4 to learn about birds' beaks.

Working out what birds eat

Discuss

You have now found out about birds' feet and beaks.
▶ Use this information to decide what type of food you
   think an owl, a gannet, a woodpecker, and a parrot
   would eat. You will be **applying** your knowledge.
▶ Use reference books to check your decisions.

Record

▶ Record your final decisions about what type of food
   you think an owl, a gannet, a woodpecker, and a
   parrot would eat.

Discuss

▶ Use what you know
   about birds to decide
   what sort of bird might
   live in this
   environment.
   Think about how it
   would walk around,
   what it might eat, and
   how it could hide. You
   will be **applying** what
   you know.

Present

▶ Design and draw a
   coloured picture of
   your bird.

Classifying

When you put things into groups because they are alike you are **classifying**. You can **classify** things in different ways. Sometimes you may use size, smell, colour, or shape to **classify**.

Classifying everyday things

The Hanlon family had a junk drawer in their kitchen. They used to throw everything into it. They decided to try to order it by dividing it into sections.

Discuss

Look at the objects in the Hanlons' drawer.
► Put them into the following groups:
  1 metal objects
  2 plastic objects
  3 paper objects
  4 any other objects.
You have now **classified** the objects.
► How useful is this **classification**?
► **Classify** the objects in more useful ways.

Record

► Make a record of your most useful **classification**.

Classifying living things

There are so many living things that it is useful to **classify** them. You can do this in different ways.

Discuss

► **Classify** the animals in Cut Out BS5 into two groups.
► What other groups can you put them into?

Record

► Make a record of how you **classified** the animals.

Classifying leaves

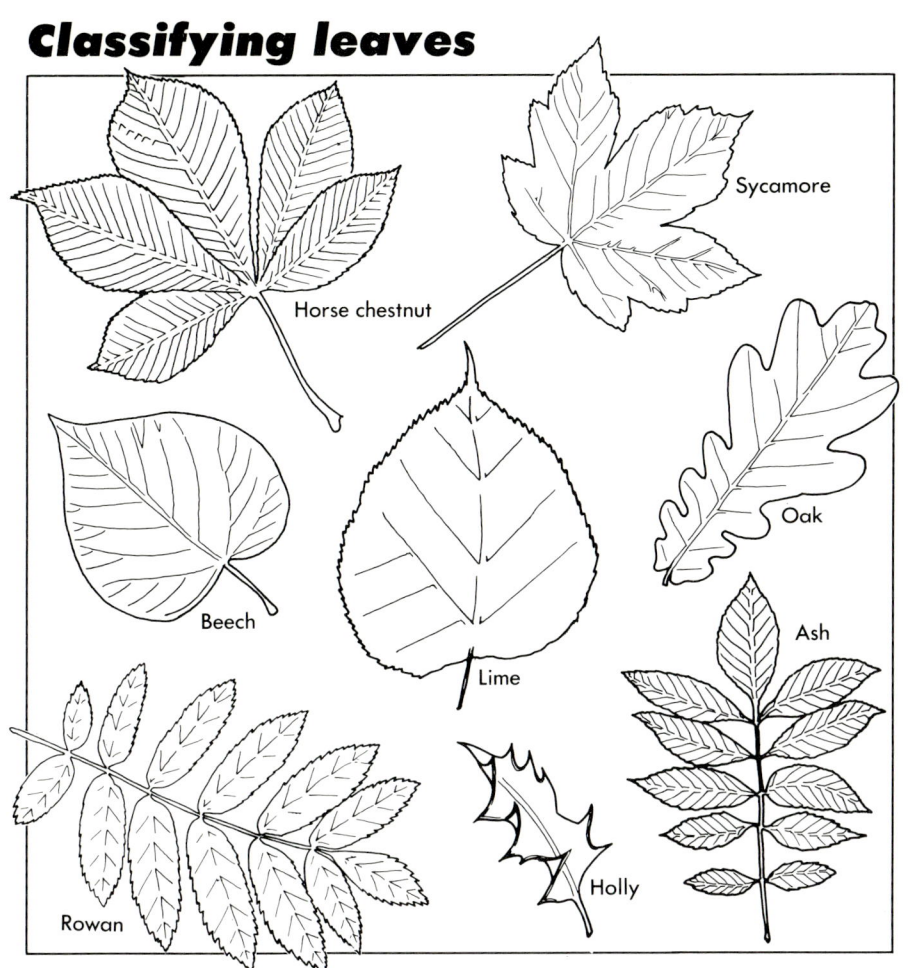

- Horse chestnut
- Sycamore
- Beech
- Lime
- Oak
- Ash
- Rowan
- Holly

Discuss

- ▶ **Classify** the leaves into two groups, those with smooth edges and those with toothed edges.

smooth edge   toothed edge

- ▶ **Classify** them into 'simple' and 'compound' leaves.

compound

simple

- ▶ How else could you **classify** them?

Using a classification key

A 'key' can be used to **classify** an unknown object. In keys, large groups are divided up into smaller groups by asking questions.

Record

- ▶ Make a record of your different **classifications**.

Discuss

- ▶ Look at the key and decide what animal X and animal Y could be.
- ▶ Make a key like this one to **classify** plants or vehicles.

Present

- ▶ Make a poster of your classification key.

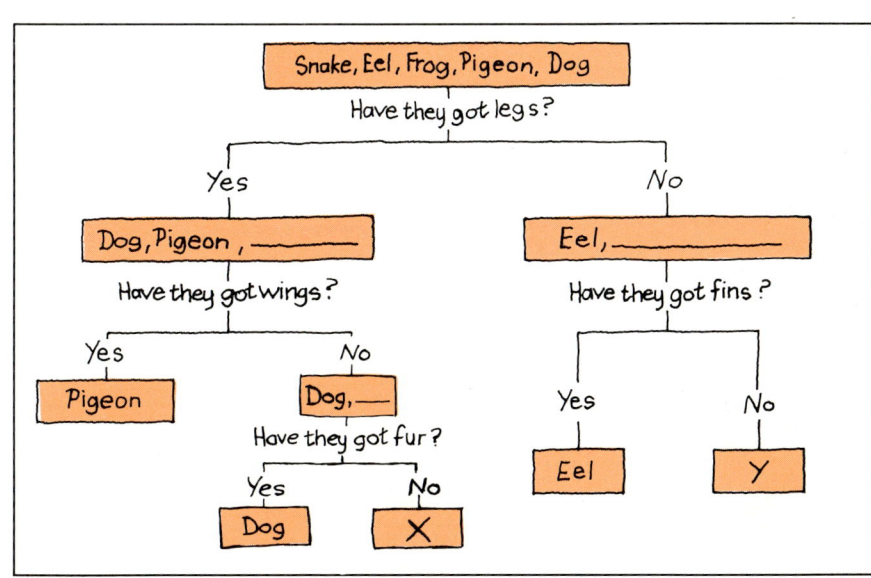

Snake, Eel, Frog, Pigeon, Dog

Have they got legs?

Yes → Dog, Pigeon, _____

No → Eel, _____

Have they got wings?

Yes → Pigeon

No → Dog, ___

Have they got fur?

Yes → Dog

No → X

Have they got fins?

Yes → Eel

No → Y

Evaluating

Evaluating means judging the activity you have just done and deciding if it was fair or if you could do it better. Carry out the activity below and then **evaluate** what you did.

Plan

Test the strength of some carrier bags.

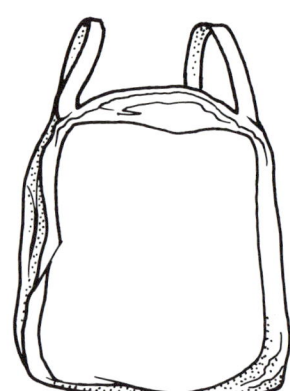
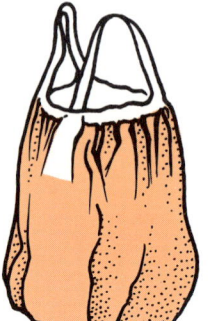
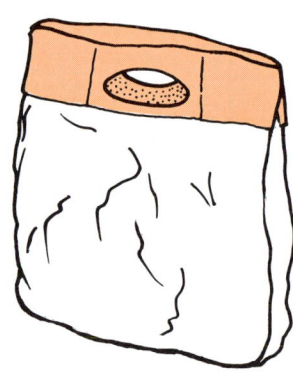

Look at the carrier bags.
Put them in the order of strength you think is correct.
- ◆ How will you test them?
- ◆ How will you record your results?

Discuss

- ▶ Discuss the questions on the checklist on the opposite page.

Record

- ▶ Make a record of what your group did.
- ▶ Use Cut Out BS6 to **evaluate** what you did.
- ▶ Make a record of ways you could improve activities you do in the future.

Checklist to evaluate your work

All the answers will be 'yes' for a perfect activity!

Did you make a safe plan for your activity?

Did your group think clearly about the idea you were setting out to test?

In your plan, did you decide what you would notice and measure?

In your plan, did you decide what you must keep the same and what you should vary to make your activity a fair test?

Did you have ideas about what you thought would happen, which you could then test?

Did you decide how to use the apparatus safely before you needed to use it?

Did you notice carefully what happened?

Did you make a suitable record?

Did you repeat the activity to check your results?

Did you discuss what you found out?

Did your results confirm your original idea, or help you change your idea to make it better?

Did your group work well as a team?

Experimenting

You will often have ideas about why something happens. When you test out your ideas you are **experimenting**. Before you **experiment**, you always predict what you think will happen. Check that you understand what 'predict' means. Spread 1.14 is about predicting.

Yvonne's group had been making different shaped boats in their CDT lessons. They had this idea:
'The speed a boat travels depends on the shape of its hull.'
The group predicted that:
'Our pointed boat will go faster than our rectangular-shaped boat.'

Plan

Plan an **experiment** to test this prediction.

Decide on some boat shapes to test. Draw them on centimetre graph paper before you cut them out.

Cut the boat shapes from a rectangle of polystyrene foam. Make sure they all weigh the same.

Leave one boat shape as a rectangle. This will give you a shape to compare the other boats with.

Check what you need to record *before* you do the **experiment**.

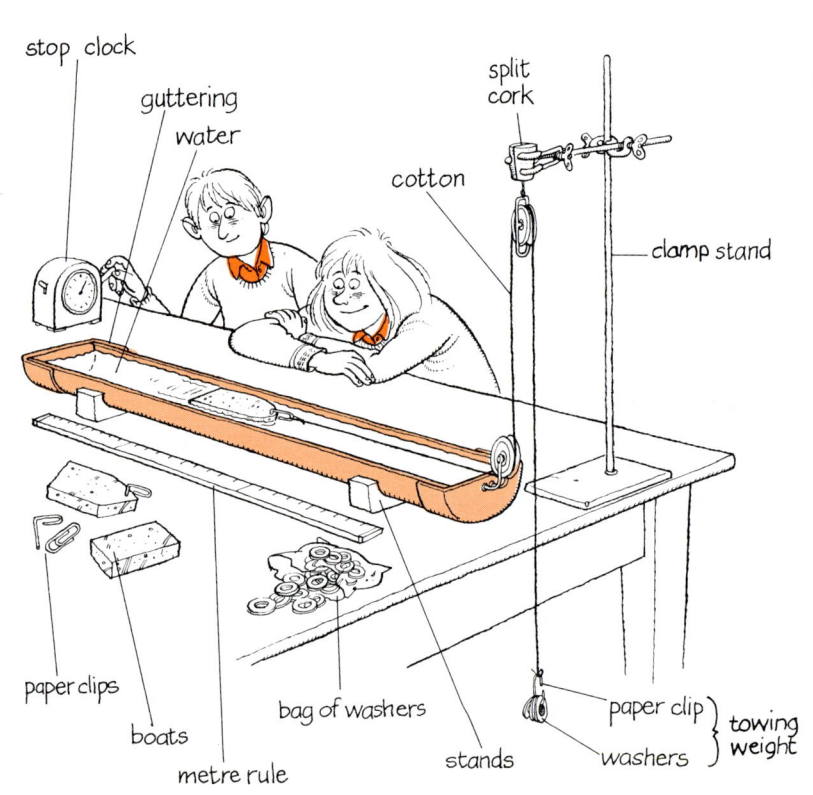

stop clock

guttering

water

split cork

cotton

clamp stand

paper clips

boats

metre rule

bag of washers

stands

paper clip

washers

towing weight

Record

▶ Draw the shapes you have made.
▶ Put the boat shapes into a list with the one you think will go fastest at the top. This is your prediction.
▶ Explain how you made all the boat shapes weigh the same.

▶ During the **experiment**, record the time each boat shape takes to travel along the gutter. Make sure you measure the same distance for each boat.
▶ After the **experiment**, record how your group's results agreed or disagreed with your previous list.

Discuss

Yvonne's group did this **experiment** too. They found out that pointed boats go faster than rectangular boats. Then they predicted that:

'Boats with pointed fronts and rounded backs go faster than boats with just pointed fronts'.

▶ Does your group agree or disagree with this idea?
▶ Test this idea if you like.

Follow the plan

Ben's group thought that the towing weights affected the speed at which the boats travelled. They decided to change the towing weight.

Predict what you think will happen.

Now test your prediction. You will be **experimenting**.

Time how long it takes to tow one of your boat shapes along the gutter. Do this three times to get a more accurate answer.

Now increase the number of weights towing the boat and repeat the test.

Take enough readings so that you can plot a graph.

➤ Shape of Boat				
Weight	Time in seconds			
Washers	1st reading	2nd reading	3rd reading	Average
0				
1	6 sec	7 sec		
2				
3				
4				
5				
6				

Record

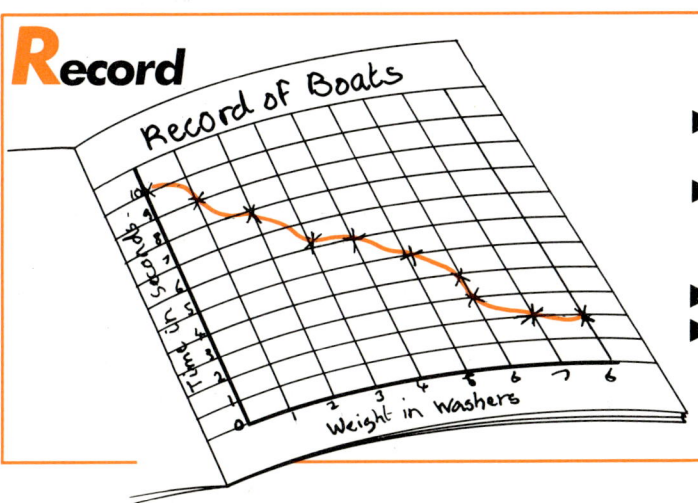

Record of Boats

Weight in Washers

▶ Make a table of results for your boat shape.
▶ Work out the average time for each trip along the gutter. Ask your teacher for help if you need it.
▶ Plot a graph (like the one on the left).
▶ Record whether your results agree or disagree with your prediction.

Hypothesizing

Making hypotheses

In science, you will often notice things happen. For example, you may notice that water from the tap on your bench flows downwards. You might then have the idea that 'water *always* flows downwards'. This idea is a **hypothesis**.

You might also have an idea which explains *why* something always happens. For example you may think 'water always flows downwards *because* gravity pulls it'. This is an even better **hypothesis**. **Hypotheses** are ideas about things which *always* happen.

Look at the diagram below. You can see Philip **hypothesizing**.

Discuss

► In your group, think of an idea which explains why milk always lasts longer in a fridge. This will be a **hypothesis**. 'Because' and 'always' are useful words to use when you **hypothesize**.

► Think of an idea which explains why ice left in a room turns to water. You will be making another **hypothesis**.

► Do you agree with Philip's **hypothesis**?

Record

► Write down or tape your group's **hypotheses**.

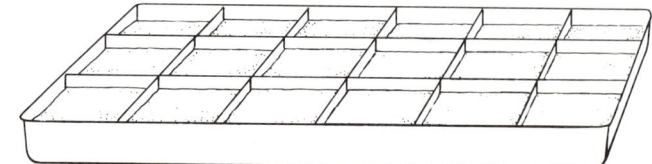

Testing hypotheses

When you have made a **hypothesis** you can test it. Usually you say what you think will happen when you do the test if your **hypothesis** is right. This is called making a prediction. The test you make is your experiment. You will find out more about predicting and experimenting in spreads 1.14 and 1.8.

Hypothesis	Prediction	Experiment
Personal stereos always play properly when they've got new batteries.	My friend's personal stereo doesn't play. It will if I put new batteries in.	Oh dear! It still doesn't work. There must be something wrong with my hypothesis.

Emma's group was finding out about paper falling to the ground. They noticed that a crumpled piece of paper fell to the ground more quickly than a flat piece. They had this idea:
'Crumpled paper always falls faster than flat paper'.
This was their **hypothesis**.

Discuss

▶ Do you agree with their **hypothesis**? If not, what ideas does your own group have?

Plan

Test Emma's group's **hypothesis**.

◆ How can you test it?
◆ What do you think will happen when you do the test?
◆ How many times will you do the test?

Record

▶ Record what you *thought* would happen.
▶ Record what *did* happen.
▶ Suggest your own **hypotheses** about the way paper falls.
▶ Try to complete this **hypothesis** 'Crumpled paper always falls faster than flat paper because ...'

Present

▶ Make a poster to explain to other people in your class how you made and tested your **hypothesis**.

Inferring

Suggest what is going on

Police are not often present at the scene of an accident so they cannot see for themselves what has happened. They have to work it out later from the evidence they find. Working out what has happened in this way is called **inferring**.

On Cut Out BS7 you will find some pictures. There are some statements about each picture too. Some of these tell you things you can actually see. These are observations. Check that you know what an observation is. If not, spread 1.13 will help you. Some of the statements try to suggest what has happened, even though you cannot see it for yourself. These statements are **inferences**.

> Two cars have crashed. This is my **observation**.

> I think that one of the drivers shot the lights. This is my **inference**.

Discuss

▶ Do the exercise on Cut Out BS7.
▶ How could you test whether your decisions were the right ones?

Inference boxes

Plan

You are now going to do some detective work of your own. Each box contains something. Without opening the box, you have to suggest what is inside it. You will be **inferring**.

Use as many senses as you can.

You may want to extend your senses and use a scientific instrument.

Think of different ways of affecting the things inside the boxes.

Only try one thing at a time.

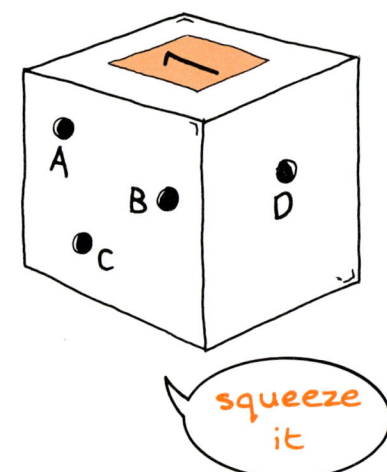

> squeeze it

> tip it
> shake it
> turn it

Record

- ▶ Make a labelled drawing of what you **inferred** about the inside of each box.
- ▶ Make a table to show what you did to each box (the cause) and what happened (the effect).
- ▶ Record which of your senses were the most useful.

Box	Cause	Effect	Senses used

Plan

- ▸ Design and build an inference box of your own. None of the sides should be longer than 10 cm.

Try your inference box on a friend.

What is inside an oil drop?

Follow the plan

You are going to make **inferences** from the way a drop of oil behaves.

Place the bowl in a tray on a flat surface and fill it with water until it overflows.

Use a ruler to push off any excess water.

Sprinkle some fine powder on top of the water.

Dip a pin into some oil so that you get a *tiny* drop on the end.

Dip this into the middle of the bowl.

Watch what happens.

Try to measure the effect with some more drops. You may need to use clean water. Or you could try a drop of detergent instead of oil.

Discuss

- ▶ What did you notice?
- ▶ Suggest what happened. You are **inferring**.
- ▸ Imagine you are an oil particle. First you are sitting in the bottle of oil. Then you find yourself inside the oil drop. What happens next?

Present

- ▸ Write a story about the oil particle's travels.
- ▸ Use drawings to show what you think is going on.

Interpreting

Interpreting means making sense of information. In science, you will **interpret** information presented in many different ways. It may be on graphs, in tables or pictures, or in words.

Interpreting at home

Below you can see some labels from clothes. Next to them is a chart which tells you what each symbol means.

Discuss

▶ Use the information in the chart to work out what the labels mean.
You are **interpreting** the information on the labels.

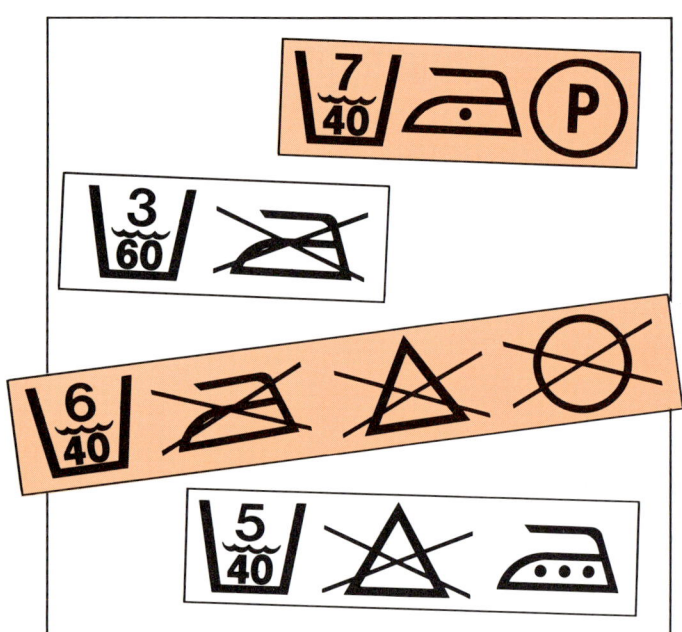

Record

▶ Draw each of the labels and write down your **interpretation** of each one.
▶ Write out the statements below and draw the correct symbol for each one.

Machine wash at 50°C.

It needs a special solvent so take it to the dry cleaners.

Use a cool iron.

Do not use bleach when you wash it.

Discuss

▶ What does this label mean?

Interpreting in science

One group tried to find out how water travels along different materials. You can see the apparatus they used in the photograph. The results they got are shown in the graph below.

Discuss

Interpret the photograph:
► What do you think the group were trying to do?
► They measured each piece of material. Why did they do this?
► What did they use the stopclock for?

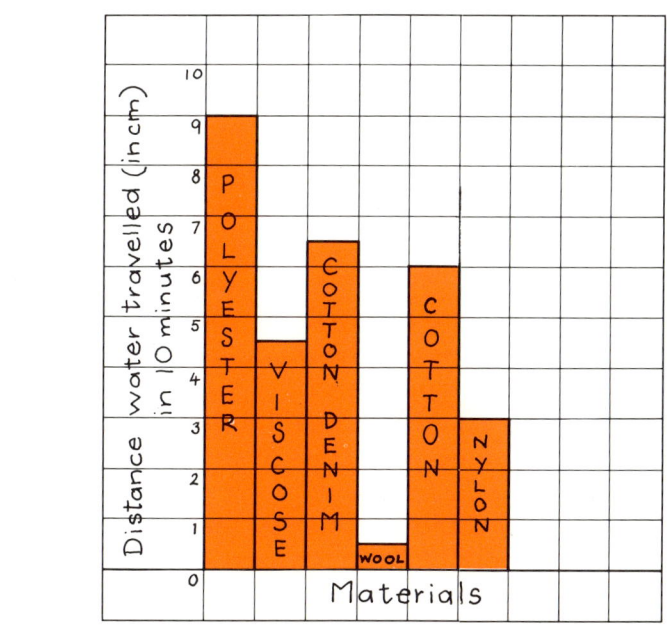

Record

► Suggest a title for this graph.
► Complete these sentences:
Water travelled furthest along ____.
Water travelled least along ____.
► Order the materials with the one in which the water moved the furthest at the top.
You have been **interpreting** the information on the graph.

Discuss

► Use the information in the graph to decide which of the ideas below you agree with. You will be **interpreting**.

Viscose and nylon materials absorb a lot of water.
Cotton materials absorb a lot of water.
Denim absorbs more water than viscose.
Cotton materials absorb less water than wool.
Polyester materials absorb less water than cotton.

► Decide how you could test each idea.

Investigating

When you **investigate**, you gather information about a topic. You can do this in a variety of ways – by using your senses to notice things, using instruments, reading, and talking to people.

Doing a survey

You are going to do a survey to find out how people choose their brand of washing-up liquid. You will be **investigating** how people choose what to buy.

Discuss

▶ Discuss some reasons why you think people buy the washing-up liquids they do. (Or, if you prefer, choose another product, such as shampoo or washing powder.)

▶ How could you find out how people choose washing-up liquids?

One way is to use a questionnaire.

▶ What questions would you ask in a questionnaire? Here are some ideas:
'Which washing-up liquid do you buy?'
'How much does it cost?'
'What do you like about it?'
'Who buys the washing-up liquid in your household?'
'Who uses it?'

Record

▶ Design your own questionnaire.

WASHING-UP LIQUID SURVEY
Number: 176
What liquid do you use?
SUPER WHIZO

Why do you buy it?
CHEAP
BUBBLY ✓
GREEN
SOFT ON HANDS ✓
BUY IN LOCAL SHOP

Plan

Now you are ready to do your survey. Your teacher will help you to duplicate your questionnaire.

◆ How could you use the questionnaire to survey your class?

◆ How could you survey the whole school?

◆ How could you survey the public? Decide with your teacher what survey to carry out.

Present

▶ Make a poster that shows the results of your surveys.
▶ Collect some empty bottles of washing-up liquid to use in your display.

Taking your investigation further

Discuss

▶ Look at some bottles of washing-up liquid and at some advertisements for them. What claims are made about each product?

▶ How do these compare with the results of your survey?

Record

▶ Decide how to record all the information you collect. A table like the one below may help you:

	Brand name	Cleano	Dazzle
claim	Smells nice	✓	
	Makes your hands soft		✓

KEEP YOUR HANDS SOFT WITH GENTLE KLEENO

Let the bubbles do the work with High Power Superclean

SUPER WHIZO IS SUPER CHEAP!

New Formula MAGIC is twice as POWERFUL

Plan

Choose one of the claims to **investigate** further.

◆ What are you going to notice or measure?
◆ What equipment do you need to carry out the **investigation**?
◆ How will you record your results?
◆ How will you make this a fair test?

Record

▶ Write down the claim you tested.
▶ Record what you did.
▶ Record what you found out during your **investigation**. Decide whether you agree with the claim.

Present

▶ Display what you have found out in a chart that the whole class can look at. You could suggest which brand you think is the best value.

Observing

When you **observe** in science, you use four of your senses to notice things: sight, touch, hearing and smell. You do not taste things in a laboratory because many chemicals are dangerous.

Plan

Use your senses to find out about each substance.

◆ What colour is it?
◆ What size is it?
◆ How does it feel?

◆ What sound does it make?
◆ What shape is it?

You are **observing**.

This smells like...

Hey, the bits are crystal-shaped.

Let's listen to the sound they make when we shake them.

Let's touch them. This one feels rough.

Let's look at the colour.

And this one feels cold.

Record

▶ Make a table of your **observations** like this one.

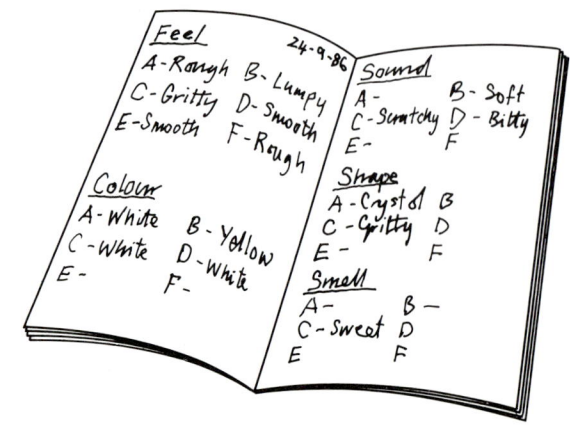

Feel   24-9-86
A-Rough   B-Lumpy   Sound
C-Gritty D-Smooth   A-   B-Soft
E-Smooth F-Rough   C-Scratchy D-Bitty
                        E-   F

Colour   Shape
A-White   B-Yellow   A-Crystal B
C-White   D-White   C-Gritty   D
E-   F-   E-   F

                        Smell
                        A-   B-
                        C-Sweet   D
                        E   F

Discuss

▶ Which **observations** would help you most if you wanted to describe the differences between the substances?

Measurement

Sometimes, in science, making **observations** with your senses is not enough. You need more accurate information, so you use measurement.

Plan

Find out about the substances you have been given by measuring them.

- We could find the mass of a bottle-top full of the substance.
- We could use a thermometer to measure their temperatures.
- Which substance will make the highest pile when it is tipped onto a piece of paper?

◆ Which measurements will you make for each substance?
◆ Did you make your measurements as accurately as possible?

Record

▶ Make a table. Draw three columns and head them 'Height of pile', 'Mass', and 'Temperature'. If you can, put the substances in order in each column.
▶ Record which measurements you think told you the most about the substances.

Changes

In science you will sometimes do things to make objects change. When you are doing this, it is important to **observe** the object before, during, and after the change. Use as many of your senses as possible. It is also very important to measure how long each change takes.

Plan

Choose one of the substances provided. Make this substance change and **observe** the changes.

Some changes

If you add water to the substances some of them fizz.

If you add vinegar to the substances some of them fizz.

If you add iodine some substances turn it black.

◆ What changes could you try. Some ideas are shown on the right.
◆ What will you measure before, during and after the change?
◆ Who will **observe** and who will record? Different people should do this.
◆ How will you time the changes to the nearest second?
◆ Try these tests on other substances.

Present

▶ Design and make a label for each substance so that when it is on a shelf it can be easily identified. Use the **observations** you have made for each substance.

Predicting

People make **predictions** all the time. The children in the picture are making a **prediction**. If they catch the bus they can feel happy with their **prediction**. If they do not catch the bus, they must think about why their **prediction** was wrong. Your **predictions** depend on the things you notice and what you already know. If you do not know anything about a situation you cannot make **predictions**. You can only make guesses.

Discuss

Here are some questions for your group to answer:

Will it rain tomorrow?
Will there be a full moon tonight?
Will school be open tomorrow?

▶ Ask each person the questions.
▶ Decide which answers they give are guesses and which are **predictions**.
▶ Make a list of some information you could collect that would help you to turn your guesses into **predictions**.
▶ Test your **predictions**.

Making a sensible guess

Sometimes, you will make a **prediction** that is wrong because something unexpected occurs. For example, you might **predict** that school will not be open on Saturday. But this particular Saturday, the school might be open for a festival. So your **prediction** would be wrong. Sometimes, you may not be able to find any information that will help you make a **prediction**. Then, you have to make a sensible guess about what you *think* will happen.

Plan

Try these activities, which both involve making **predictions**.
You can do either one first.

Fill your container to the top with water.

Predict how many 1p coins you think you will be able to put into the bowl before it overflows.

Test your **prediction**.

◆ Can you give a reason for what you noticed?
◆ Would you expect a similar result with a tall, narrow, glass container?

Container A contains small marbles.
Container B contains large marbles.

Predict which container, A or B, you think will need more water to cover the marbles.

Test your **prediction**.

Make sure you measure the amount of water you pour in.

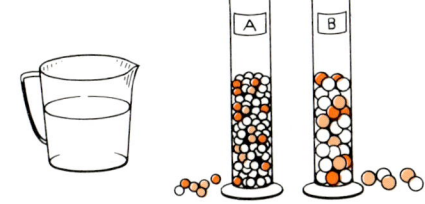

◆ What do you think would happen if you used sand instead of marbles?

When you test **predictions** you are experimenting. You can find out more about experimenting on spread 1.8.

Discuss

Look at the table which shows the average height and weight of all the students in the first four years of a secondary school. Four readings have been left out.
▶ **Predict** where they should be placed in the table.

Age	Boys height (cm)	Girls height (cm)	Boys weight (kg)	Girls weight (kg)
11	144	145	35	36
12		152		40
13	155	158	42	
14	163		49	49

38	150	45	160

Questioning

You will often need to ask **questions** to find out more about something you want to understand. Asking **questions** can help you to notice things and decide what sort of tests to do.

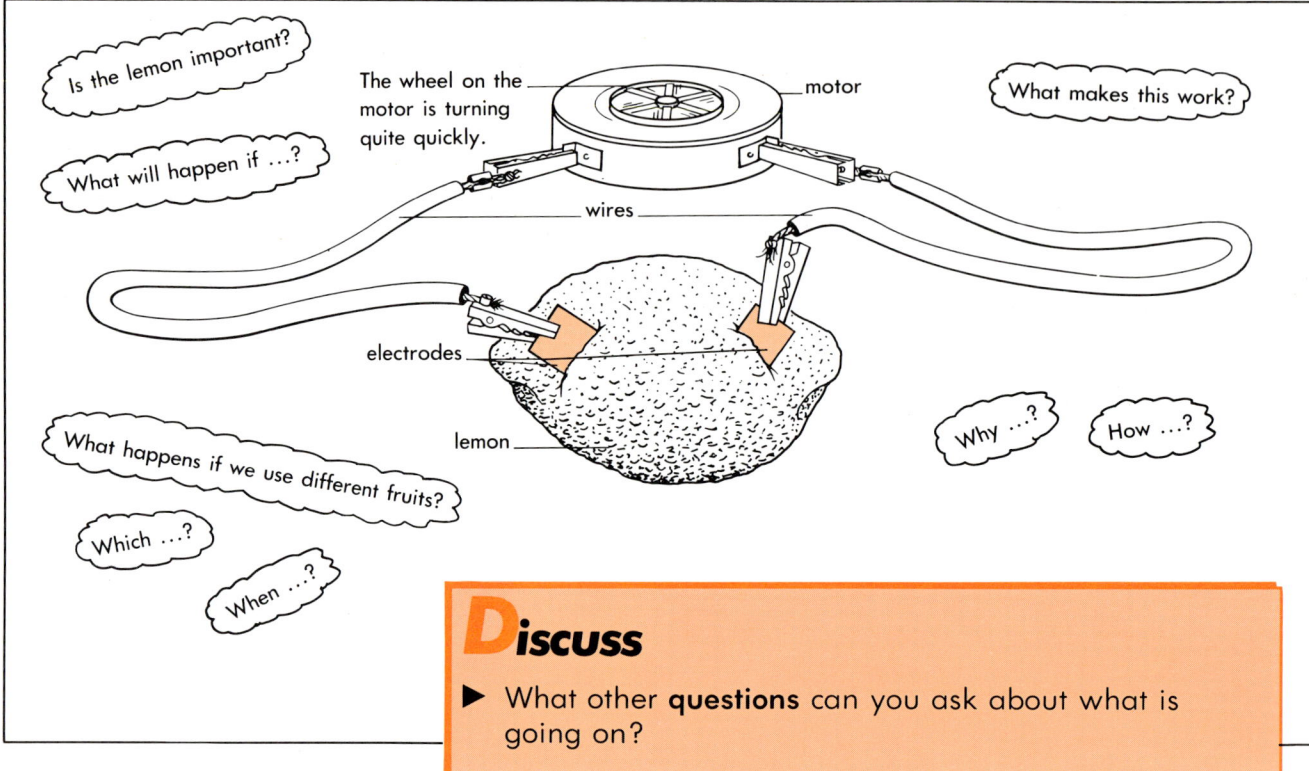

Is the lemon important?

The wheel on the motor is turning quite quickly.

motor

What makes this work?

What will happen if …?

wires

Why …?

How …?

electrodes

lemon

What happens if we use different fruits?

Which …?

When …?

Discuss

▶ What other **questions** can you ask about what is going on?

Electricity from a lemon

Which part of the lemon is needed to make electricity? Before you can find the answer to this **question**, you will need to ask other **questions**.

Plan

Find out which part of the lemon is used to make electricity. Use the questions below to help you.

◆ Does the motor turn when the electrodes are in the lemon skin?

◆ Does the motor turn when the electrodes are in the juice?

Record

▶ Make a record of what you did.
▶ Record the answer to the **question** 'Which part of the lemon is needed to make electricity?'

Electricity from other juices

In the investigation you have just done, you were given some **questions** to help you. Now you are going to try asking your own **questions**. One **question** you could ask is:
'Can you produce electricity using other juices?'

Discuss

▶ In your group, discuss this **question**.
▶ What do you think the answer is?
▶ What **questions** can you ask to find out more?
  Here are some examples:
  Will it work with vinegar?
  Will it work with water?

Plan

Find out if electricity can be produced using other juices.
◆ What **questions** do you need to ask?

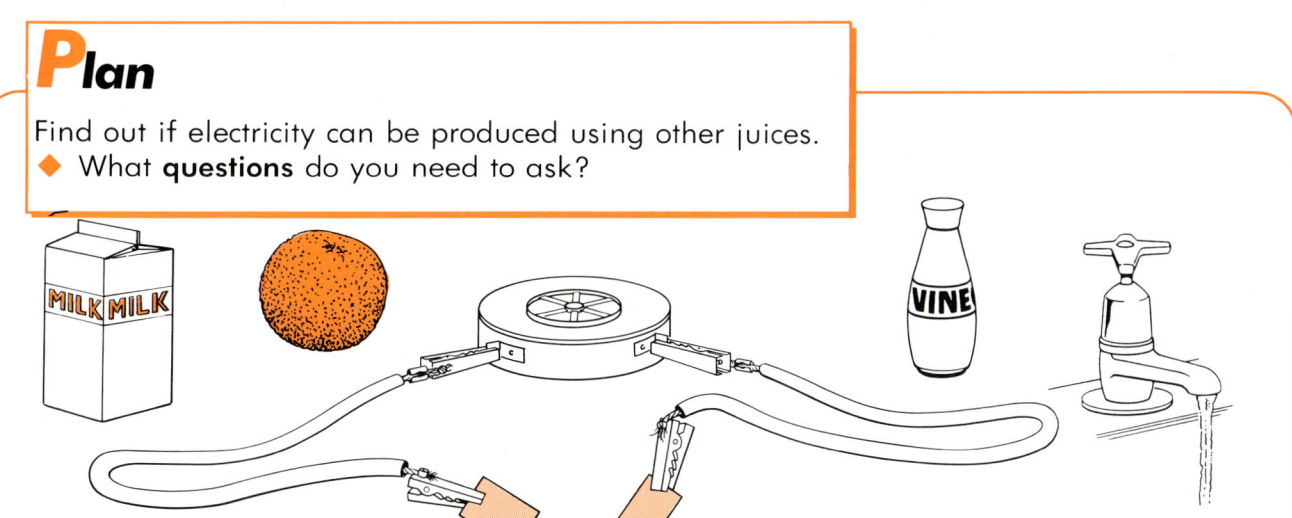

Plan

Read the **questions** below.

◆ Is the distance between the electrodes important?
◆ Is the size of the electrodes important?
◆ Does it matter which way round you connect the motor?
◆ Does it work if the electrodes are the same?

Choose one of the **questions** and find out the answer to it. Ask other **questions** to help you find out more.

Record

▶ Make a record of what you did.
▶ Record your group's answer to the **question** you chose.
▶ Record the **questions** that your group found useful.
▶ Make a list of other **questions** you could ask that could help you find out more about the lemon and electricity.

Be scientific
—some useful words

accurate

apparatus

apply

assess

astronomy

attitude

belief

biology

book

change

checking

chemistry

civilization

classify

communicate

compare

computer

conclusion

constant

control

cooperation

creative

critical

culture

curiosity

data

decide

discuss

encyclopaedia

engineer

enquire

error

evaluate

exact

experiment

explain

explore

fact

find out

forensic

geology

help

honest

hypothesis

idea

independence

infer

information

interact

interpret

invention

investigate

know

listen

logic

manipulate

measure

method

mistake

model

natural

observe

open-minded

opinion

original

pattern

persevere

physics

plan

precise

predict

present

problem solving

process

question

read

record

relationships

repeat

research

responsibility

science

scientific

scientist

self-criticism

skill

standard

technology

theory

thinking

truth

unbiased

understanding

universal

useful

variable